Simply Existing

Samantha Gaspari

BookLeaf Publishing

Presentation by *BookLeaf Publishing*

Web: www.bookleafpub.com

E-mail: info@bookleafpub.com

ISBN: 9789395756419

First edition 2022

ACKNOWLEDGEMENT

Thank you to the family and friends that have always supported me. I honestly would not be here without you. To the people that continue to push and nurture my creativity: I appreciate you.

PREFACE

Warning:

The contents of this book showcase intense emotions that may be difficult for some to read. Please proceed with caution regarding the following topics: anxiety, depression, and self harm. Always remember, it is okay to not be okay, but know you can seek help when needed.

The Girl I Was Before

I often wonder
what 13-year-old me would think
if she saw us now
Somehow I doubt she would be proud
I can almost hear her
screaming from the void

Being Consumed

There was nothing I could do at the time
I felt helpless
I could sense the demons
being unleashed inside my head
ripping apart my heart
and filling every crevice of myself
with darkness

Hopelessness

The waves crash down
upon the fragile coastline
in the same way my hope did
A slow rise
A sudden shift
A final break
A cascading descent
Wearing away the sand
in the same way
it eroded my happiness

Depression

There are tissues scattered in the bed
Used ones and new ones
but I can't seem to tell the difference
I don't think it matters much anyway
I just need something to catch the tears
I think my pillowcase has had enough
It's been soaking up my pain all week
and I can feel my eyes growing tired
like they're begging for a break
I know I've been pleading for one too

The Garden

5

Anxiety sprouts
from the soil of fear
and grows with panic
The flowers don't bloom
because the roots have all been poisoned
The vines constrict
as they wrap around your life
until you're lost
in your own garden

Glass Heart

The heart shatters
like glass
Broken down
into minuscule shards
of pain and despair

Pill Bottles

I woke up today
I don't know if that's luck
or misfortune
when I spent the whole night
begging for this pain to end
And each time I reach the bottom
of these fluorescent orange bottles
I still can't seem to convince myself
that maybe this life
is worth something

When Will It End

I don't recall the amount of hours spent
hiding beneath the blankets on the bed
But my pillowcase was soaked with tears
and my head was pounding
while my eyes were burning
I just wanted it to stop
The pain. The crying. Life
I just wanted it all to end

Self Destruction

The mind and body wage wars against
themselves
shown in crimson crescent scars down our arms
What about self destruction seems so appealing?
It's simply the thought of creating any amount of
pain
just to evade the one eating away at my soul

I Just Want to Sleep

I am tired
but not in the way you might think
All I feel is this impending sense of doom
and I know that I need to get out of bed
because I haven't eaten or showered
but the sheets feel too heavy
like my thoughts weighing me down
I keep forcing myself to sleep
just to escape the pain
and I can't seem to understand
why I keep waking up

How it Feels

I have come to learn that anxiety
takes over your entire body and mind
No matter what you do
or where you go
there is always that voice
in the back of your mind
controlling you from the inside
shadowing over every thought
It's a feeling of dread
Of worry
Of doubt
This internal darkness envelopes your soul
keeping you from doing what you want
and from feeling how you want to feel

Critical

My insecurities could eat me alive
but I don't think anyone would notice
if they swallowed me whole
because I feel trapped within a body
that forgets to eat
often lacks the ability to sleep
and cares too much about what other people
think
Except I know that if it's anything like what I see
I cannot blame them for not liking me
when I struggle every day
just to attempt to like myself

Panic Attack

My breathing came in short pants
unable to inhale any substantial amount of
oxygen
and my feet curl under me
as I wrap my sweatshirt over my head and
around my body
and sharp pains shoot through my chest
and my throat tightens as my heart pounds
and tears race down my face
and I become dizzy as my vision turns black
and I force my eyes shut but I can't breathe
and instinct tells me to run
so I jump out of my seat
and make a break for the door
but outside I crumple to the ground
head between my knees
trying to obtain any semblance of breath
But I just can't breathe

Then and Now

How did I go from skinned knees on the
playground
to red crescent lines down my arms in the
bathroom
From discarded candy bar wrappers in the
kitchen
to empty orange bottles on the countertops
You don't realize you're slipping away from
yourself
away from the laughter and careless freedom of
innocence
until you're consumed within the darkness
And one day you notice almost suddenly
you've gone from broken bones to scattered
ashes
of the girl you once used to be

Brain Fog

Sometimes I am lost
within the thick fog
inside my brain
and I feel like I am drowning
within this humidity
So please bear with me
while I choke my way out

Changing Seasons

Even in the silent depths
of a frigid winter morning
the sunrise spills over the horizon
Not to wrap the earth
within its warm embrace
but to reassure the soul
that soon the bleakness will break
and spring will prosper

To Become Whole Again

Despite being fragile
and feeling fractured
worn down
torn apart
broken
I know deep down
within these scattered fragments
of my soul
I am the only one
that holds the glue
and has the capability
of working delicately enough
to put the pieces back together

An Ode to My Youth

If I could reach within the depths of my ribcage
to hug you
I would not hesitate
And I would express to you
just how truly sorry I am
For not sticking up for you
For being consumed with the notion
we would never be enough
For sacrificing us at the expensive
of making everyone else happy
But most importantly
I am sorry for abandoning you
For becoming lost within the shadows
when you needed me most

Surviving

The sky blends reds and blues upon sunrise
as it spills over the horizon
in the same way it melds hope and warmth
throughout the soul
In a way to remind us
that if we can survive through the darkness
there will always be light that follows

Mirror

My mirror has heard
more insults than compliments
And every vicious word
has broken off a shard of glass
over the years
And maybe its a silly superstition
but I've come to that realization
that to break a mirror
means seven years of bad luck
and hating myself continues to accumulate
So to keep the mirror whole
or even to glue it back together
maybe I need to love myself
just a little bit more

Beauty Within

It's time you found your beauty
Learn to let it unfold and develop
into the best version of yourself
You may be fragile or scarred
holding onto yourself too tightly
just to prevent inevitably falling apart
But know you can heal what is broken
You are the fire lit on a frigid night
A light within the darkness
A hug after absence
The smell before rain
You don't have to forget the pain
But you can grow from it
As a vine among thorns
climbing the lattice of life
It is only within the weeds
you'll find the beauty within yourself